PIONEERS

Troll Associates

PIONEERS

by Francene Sabin

Illustrated by Hal Frenck

Troll Associates

Library of Congress Cataloging in Publication Data

Sabin, Francene.
  Pioneers.

  Summary: Traces the westward movement of settlers
from the original thirteen American colonies into the
wilderness beyond the Appalachian Mountains.
    1. Pioneers—West (U.S.)—History—Juvenile literature.
2. Frontier and pioneer life—West (U.S.)—Juvenile
literature. 3. West (U.S.)—History—Juvenile literature.
[1. Pioneers. 2. Frontier and pioneer life. 3. West
(U.S.)—History] I. Frenck, Hal, ill. II. Title.
F596.S14   1984   978   84-2580
ISBN 0-8167-0120-2 (lib. bdg.)
ISBN 0-8167-0121-0 (pbk.)

Even before the Revolutionary War ended and the United States of America came into being, some colonists were looking west to the frontier.

For these hardy pioneers, the colonies, with their still-small populations, ·had become too crowded and too civilized. The same dreams that had brought them and their parents to the New World were luring them into the wilderness beyond the Appalachian Mountains.

The pioneers were a widely mixed lot. They were trappers and farmers, hunters and shopkeepers, missionaries hoping to convert the Indians, and criminals running away from the law. They were scholars and artists, adventurers and visionaries. They traveled west for cheap or free farm land, for gold or fur pelts, or for the chance to trade with the Indians.

Some, like the Mormons, hoped to establish settlements where they could practice their religion in peace. Some, like Daniel Boone or the mountain men, couldn't bear to settle down.

There were dozens of reasons for going out west into the wilderness. But one thing united all the pioneers: it was the willingness to take up the challenge of the frontier.

Some historians divide the movement west into three successive waves. The first wave took place in the mid-1700s. It did not involve a large number of people. That was because the area west of the Appalachian Mountains was, until 1763, the scene of a series of battles known as the French and Indian War. Then, when the war ended, the British government prohibited the colonists from settling in the area.

The second westward wave began about the time of the Revolution and lasted roughly sixty years. During this period, the pioneers pushed the frontier as far as the Mississippi River.

The last wave began during the 1830s and spanned about twenty years. During this time, the pioneers extended the frontier to the Pacific Ocean. By the mid-1800s, the railroads and the telegraph had opened the West to business, easy travel, and a more civilized way of life. But for the early pioneers, the going was rough and often dangerous.

The rich lands and forests of Kentucky were the goals of the first pioneers. In the mid-1700s, only a few people had actually seen this area. But it was praised throughout the New World and Europe as an earthly paradise. The stories made it sound so tempting that even the rugged mountains and uncharted forests couldn't stop the pioneers from setting out for "old Caintuck."

Led by Daniel Boone and other trail-blazers, the pioneers struggled over the Appalachians. There were no roads or bridges. They had to chop their way through forests to get their small supply wagons past the trees. They had to build rafts to carry their possessions across rivers. Some days the going was so rough that they didn't cover more than a mile.

Anything the pioneers could make with their own hands was left behind. But they did take iron utensils, such as a corn grater, a large cooking pot, a kettle, a three-legged skillet, and a long fork and ladle.

The pioneers also brought basic tools, such as axes, saws, hoes, plows, hammers and anvils, knives, rifles, and molds for making bullets. If the family owned a featherbed, it went along. So did extra clothing, blankets, pewter plates, a few pieces of china, and a clock.

Most of the pioneers who moved west were farmers. Their first task in the wilderness was to get a piece of land. They bought their farm site from a land company or from the government. In both cases it was very inexpensive.

Still, the cost of land, which was never more than two dollars an acre, was beyond what some farmers could afford. So these pioneers simply settled on a piece of public land and began working it. People who didn't own the property they lived on were called squatters. Later, under squatter's rights, they were able to buy the land very cheaply from the government.

The best farm land was fairly flat, not too rocky, and near a stream. Whenever possible, pioneer families settled rather close together. It was important to have neighbors. In case of Indian attacks, the settlers banded together to fight off the attackers.

Neighbors also joined forces to clear big rocks and tree stumps, to build houses, to husk corn, to make quilts, and to do all the other tasks that couldn't be done by one family.

The jobs the neighbors did as a group became occasions for parties. For example, it usually required three days to build a log cabin. During that time all the families ate together and enjoyed shooting contests, races, dancing, and other activities. Most of the time frontier life was hard and lonely, and the pioneers looked forward to these neighborly gatherings.

Wherever several families settled, they also built a fort. The first forts were just large, flat areas, usually on a hill. They were enclosed by stockades, or log walls that stood ten to twelve feet high.

Later, blockhouses were built in the corners of the stockades. They had rifle slits through which the settlers fired at attacking Indians. There were also a few small cabins built along the inside of the stockade. Newcomers to the area lived in these cabins until they could build their own homes.

Pioneers tried to reach their homestead and get the land cleared before planting time in the spring. Nothing was more important than being able to harvest enough food for the coming winter. So the first spring and summer were spent doing little else except working the land.

Meanwhile, the family lived in an open lean-to called a half-camp. It was like a wooden shed with an open side that faced the fire, which was used to cook, to provide warmth, and to frighten off wild animals.

The main crop of most pioneer families was corn. It was eaten at every meal—as corn-on-the-cob, as hominy, or ground up and made into bread, pancakes, and cereal.

The farmers also had vegetable gardens, sheep, a dairy cow or two, a few chickens, and hogs. Until the first crop was harvested, however, the newcomers often had to live on roots and berries and nuts from the forest. And, of course, wild game was a plentiful and important part of the frontier diet.

After the first harvest and before winter set in, the pioneers built their one-room, log-cabin homes. Once the cabin was up, they furnished it with a homemade split-log table and benches, and built a flatboard bed into one corner of the room. Parents slept on this, using a soft featherbed, if they had one. If not, they slept on a pile of dry leaves or cornhusks covered with deerskins.

Pioneer clothing was mostly handmade. Flax, grown on the farm, was spun into linen. This was then combined with wool the pioneers sheared from their own sheep, to make a cloth called linsey-woolsey.

Linsey-woolsey and deerskins were used for nearly all the clothing worn on the frontier. Spinning and weaving cloth were among the tasks done when the day's work

ended or the weather was bad. The pioneers also made footwear for the winter, repaired tools, and molded rifle bullets. Clearly, there was not much time for relaxing.

Once an area was well established, the pioneers built a one-room schoolhouse and a church. Then they hired a teacher, who was paid by being given room and board in one neighborhood home after another.

Until the settlers could afford to pay a full-time preacher, services were conducted by a traveling preacher. He would visit for a few days, perform marriages, baptisms, and any other services requiring a clergyman.

In time, a settlement acquired stores, a law officer, and other forms of civilization. But by then, the more restless pioneers had moved farther west.

As they moved across the midwestern plains, the pioneers rode in vehicles called Conestoga wagons. The Conestoga wagon had a high, round, canvas covering. It was big enough to carry a family, food and supplies for the long trip, and necessities for the new home that would be built in Oregon or California.

By the 1840s, the jumping-off point for the wagon trains of pioneers was Independence, Missouri. Here, a large group of families would join together under a leader they elected.

But even more important than the leader was the scout hired to lead them over the Oregon Trail and north to the Willamette Valley in Oregon, or southwest over the Santa Fe Trail.

The scouts, such as Kit Carson and Jim Bridger, were also called pilots. They were the only ones who had actually been through the wilderness. They knew when to hit the trail, how fast to travel, what to take, where to find food and water, and how to avoid trouble with the Indians. Wagon trains that ignored the advice of their scouts often ended in tragedy, with many of the pioneers dying in the arid desert or the snow-filled mountains, or being wiped out by Indian raiding parties.

Yet nothing—neither hardship, nor disappointment, nor death—could stop the movement west. The dream of the frontier was stronger than its threats and dangers. And the age of the pioneer didn't end until there was no frontier left to conquer.